W9-BXW-940

GAME DAY
RED SOX BASEBALL

GAME DAY
RED SOX BASEBALL

**The Greatest Games, Players, Managers and Teams
in the Glorious Tradition of Red Sox Baseball**

TRIUMPH
B O O K S
CHICAGO

Athlon® Sports™
AMERICA'S PREMIER SPORTS ANNUALS

Library of Congress Control Number: 2005910954

This book is available in quantity at special discounts for your group or organization.
For further information, contact:

Triumph Books
542 South Dearborn Street
Suite 750
Chicago, Illinois 60605
(312) 939-3330
Fax (312) 663-3557

WRITER: Tyler Kepner

EDITORS: Rob Doster, Mitchell Light

PHOTO EDITOR: Tim Clark
PHOTO ASSISTANT: Maurice Hopkins

DESIGN: Anderson Thomas Design

PHOTO CREDITS: Getty Images, AP/Wide World, Major League Baseball, National Baseball Hall of Fame

Printed in U.S.A.

ISBN-13: 978-1-57243-836-1
ISBN-10: 1-57243-836-3

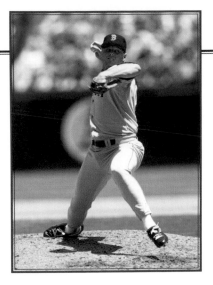

CONTENTS

Foreword

Through the years, I've been labeled "Mr. Red Sox." Now I don't know if that is true or not, but I do know I've been honored to be a part of this team for more than 60 years.

The Boston Red Sox are a special club, and their fans are second to none. The atmosphere in Boston is unmatched. People talk about places like St. Louis and New York and Chicago, but there is nothing like Boston. There is some sort of mystique there.

It all starts with Fenway Park. The new owners have done so much since they've taken over, it is like a brand new ballpark. They've added a lot of seats, but I think they need to add some more. Fenway Park is a perfect setting, but the fans are so gung-ho about the Red Sox, they could move the seating capacity up to forty thousand—no problem. I see a lot of the same families at the park year after year, and they just love the Red Sox.

One of my proudest moments of being with the Red Sox was on Opening Day in 2005, when I was able to raise the World Series championship banner in center field. The old captain, Carl Yastrzemski, raised it with me, and the fans were terrific. I also remember Joe

Torre having his team up on the top step when I received my ring. That meant a lot to me.

That day was a true celebration of that 2004 club and all it accomplished. That club had the best combination I've ever seen of good players and good guys pulling for each other. Kevin Millar, Bill Mueller, Johnny Damon, Tim Wakefield. They really cared for each other, and that started with David Ortiz and Manny Ramirez. Just a wonderful group.

Being in the locker room in St. Louis was great. I never saw so many happy guys crying in my whole life, and I was one of them. It was a big thrill and truly overwhelming. Even the new guys to the Red Sox appreciated what it meant. They were all acting like children, and I couldn't blame them.

Playing with Ted Williams was the highlight of my career. He was the greatest hitter who ever lived, and the numbers back him up. Certainly there have been other hitters, but no one like Ted. He had the average, the power, and he lost years on his career to two wars.

The game is certainly changing, but the future is bright for the Red Sox. I feel privileged to be part of this organization for so long, and my hope is to continue to be a part of it for as long as I can.

—JOHNNY PESKY

Introduction

The images are unforgettable and too numerous to count.

Ted Williams, bringing a scientist's approach and a surgeon's precision to the plate, and hitting a baseball like no one before or since. Carl Yastrzemski taking Teddy Ballgame's place in left field and placing his own stamp of determined excellence on the franchise. Carlton Fisk. Roger Clemens and Pedro Martinez after him, bringing the electricity of a rock concert to Fenway Park. Roberts, Big Papi and the bloody sock.

And yes, there are the losses, the moments of epic frustration and despair. Too many, and too painful, to mention here. But they are part of the unique fabric of Red Sox Nation. We're taking the history, drama and pageantry of Boston Red Sox baseball and distilling them into the pages that follow. It's a daunting task. No other baseball team inspires the loyalty and passion that the Red Sox elicit from their fans.

Through the words and images we present, we hope you will get a taste of what the Boston Red Sox are all about. Decades have passed since players first donned the red and blue, but one thing hasn't changed: Red Sox baseball is a way of life.

TRADITIONS AND PAGEANTRY

The sights and sounds of Game Day in Boston create an unmatched spectacle, a glorious mix of tradition and color and pomp and pageantry. Here's a small sample of what makes the Boston Red Sox unique among all professional sports franchises.

Fenway Park

The Red Sox' first home was a wooden structure called Huntington Avenue Grounds, now part of Northeastern University. They played their first game at Fenway Park just days after the *Titanic* sunk, on April 20, 1912, beating the New York Highlanders (as the Yankees were then known) 7–6 in 11 innings. The Detroit Tigers opened their park the same day, and for years, Fenway Park and Tiger Stadium were the oldest facilities in baseball. Now, Fenway stands alone as the oldest, an authentic time capsule with just a few inconveniences, such as poles blocking fans' line of vision. It is the smallest park in the majors, with a capacity of 35,095 for night games, and fans adore it. The Red Sox set attendance records each year from 2000 to 2005, and their home helped inspire the new generation of ballparks that seek to recreate the quirks and charm that come naturally at The Fens.

The Green Monster

At first, there was more than just a 37-foot Monster towering above 228 feet of left field at Fenway Park. From 1912 to 1933, there was a 10-foot slope leading up to the wall, known as "Duffy's Cliff" after Sox left fielder Duffy Lewis. Owner Tom Yawkey ordered the ground flattened in 1934, but the wall stayed— there was no other choice. Landsdowne St. borders that side of Fenway Park, and a tall wall was the only way to keep home runs from pelting the street. It remains an inviting target, not just for homers but for doubles; many left-handed hitters have taken advantage of the Green Monster for two-base hits. The

Wall was first made of wood, then covered in tin and eventually hard plastic, with a ladder in play near the top. Under the Red Sox' new ownership, the team has added seating atop the Monster and expanded the famous hand-operated scoreboard to include the AL East standings (and more advertisements). The initials—in Morse code—of Thomas A. Yawkey and Jean R. Yawkey appear in vertical stripes on the scoreboard, and red and blue lights

record balls, strikes and outs. The bottom of the wall includes padding, which was added after Fred Lynn hurt himself in a collision with the wall in the 1975 World Series.

"I loved having that thing behind me." CARL YASTRZEMSKI ON THE GREEN MONSTER

The Red Seat

Every day at Fenway Park, a fan sits in Section 42, Row 37, Seat 21, and might wonder why that seat is red, in contrast to every other bleacher seat. The explanation dates to June 9, 1946, when Ted Williams hit the longest home run ever to land in the ballpark. Williams' clout, off Fred Hutchinson of the Detroit Tigers, is said to have traveled 502 feet and broken through the straw hat of the fan sitting in that seat.

The Nickname

In the early days of the franchise, the Red Sox went by several nicknames. The 1901 team was known as the Americans, the 1902 version went by Somersets, and the teams from 1903 to 1906 were known as the Pilgrims. In 1907, owner John I. Taylor changed the name to the Red Sox, and that is the name that stuck.

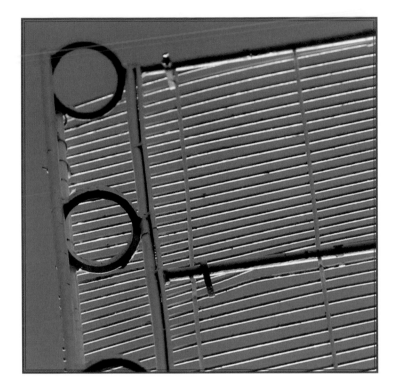

——— Pesky Pole ———

While right field at Fenway Park juts abruptly to a distance of 380 feet, the foul pole in the corner is actually just 302 feet from the plate. It is named for Johnny Pesky, the Sox icon who played shortstop for the team in the '40s and '50s. Pesky batted left-handed and hit just six home runs in his career at Fenway, but one of them wrapped around the foul pole to win a game for Mel Parnell, who dubbed it "Pesky's Pole." In Game 1 of the 2004 World Series, Mark Bellhorn's eighth-inning drive hit the pole and won the game for the Sox.

Celebrity Fans

No team in baseball seems to inspire a more loyal celebrity following than the Boston Red Sox. Author Stephen King, actors Ben Affleck and Matt Damon and singers James Taylor and Steven Tyler are frequent guests at Fenway Park. In the 2003 playoffs, Affleck brought Jennifer Lopez with him. By 2005, it was his new bride, Jennifer Garner, by his side. Damon has watched games from the broadcast booth with Jerry Remy; King once included a Red Sox pitcher, Tom Gordon, in the title of a novel; and Taylor and Tyler have sung the national anthem at Fenway.

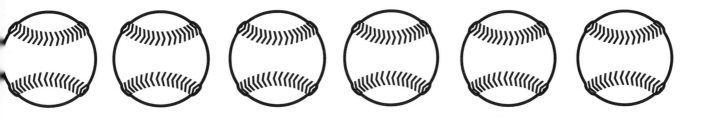

Retired numbers

For years, the Red Sox had a strict policy on retiring uniform numbers. There were three guidelines: the player must be a member of the Baseball Hall of Fame, must have compiled at least 10 years of service to the Red Sox, and must have finished his career with the team. The first four players honored—Ted Williams (9), Joe Cronin (4), Bobby Doerr (1) and Carl Yastrzemski (8)—met those criteria. In 2000, the Sox bent the rule and retired Carlton Fisk's No. 27 after his election to the Hall of Fame. Fisk played 11 seasons with the Red Sox but finished his career with the White Sox. Given Fisk's enduring popularity in his native New England, nobody complained.

Horner
Photo

THE GREAT RED SOX

The Sox may have sold baseball's greatest player, but Sox history didn't end with Babe Ruth. The Sox' all-time roster boasts the greatest assortment of baseball legends this side of Cooperstown, including the Greatest Hitter Who Ever Lived.

———— Hall of Famers ————

JIMMY COLLINS

According to his plaque in Cooperstown, third baseman Jimmy Collins "revolutionized the style of play at that bag" with defense that "thrilled fans of both major leagues." It also mentions Collins' most valuable contribution to the Red Sox: his membership on the 1903 champions. Collins was the Red Sox' player-manager in the first six years of the American League franchise, and before that, he played six seasons for the Boston Beaneaters of the National League. Renowned for his ability to field a bunt at third base, Collins finished his career with 1,999 hits and a .294 average. As a manager, he led the Red Sox to a 455–376 record and two pennants.

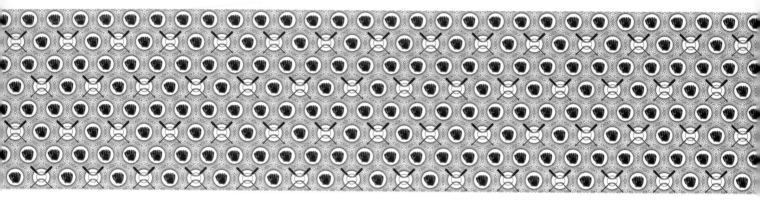

CY YOUNG

Denton True "Cy" Young started his career in 1890, three years before the mound was moved back to 60 feet, 6 inches. His first nine years were with the soon-to-be defunct Cleveland Spiders, and after two more years in the National League with St. Louis, Young jumped to the Boston entry in the new American League. Already the owner of 286 victories, Young was an instant sensation, winning 33 and 32 games his first two seasons and throwing the first pitch in World Series history in 1903. Young won twice in that Series, and punctuated his 1904 campaign with a perfect game on May 5. Young would win 192 games for the Sox, and his career totals in wins, losses, innings and complete games are easily the most in baseball history. The award that bears his name was first given out in 1956, the year after his death.

TRIS SPEAKER

When the Red Sox opened Fenway Park in 1912, their biggest hitting star was Tris Speaker, who batted .383 that year, leading the American League in doubles (53) and home runs (10). A member of Boston's "Million Dollar Outfield," Speaker helped the Red Sox win two championships. Shipped to Cleveland in 1916 for two players and $55,000, Speaker would beat out Ty Cobb for the batting title that season and win the 1920 World Series as the Indians' player-manager. Speaker is the major leagues' career leader in doubles, with 792, but he also specialized in taking doubles away. Speaker played shallow in center and used his speed and instincts to make him, according to his Hall of Fame plaque, the "greatest center fielder of his day."

HARRY HOOPER

The only player to win four championships with the Red Sox is Harry Hooper, the leadoff man and fine defensive right fielder on the 1912, 1915, 1916 and 1918 teams. Hooper is the Red Sox career leader in triples (130) and stolen bases (300), and though he hit only 75 career homers, he had notable moments of power. Hooper was the first player to hit two homers in a World Series game, victimizing the Phillies in the Game 5 clincher in 1915. He is also the first player to lead off both games of a double-header with a home run, in 1913.

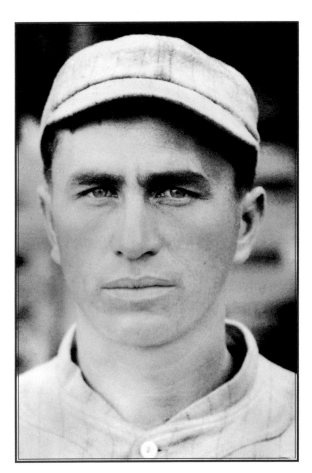

BABE RUTH

In any other business, the Red Sox would have been hailed for their skill in the buying and selling of Babe Ruth. They plucked him from the minor league Baltimore Orioles in 1914 for less than $40,000, and sold him to the Yankees six years later for $125,000. But, alas, Ruth was not a stock—he was an incandescent ballplayer whose departure is said to have cursed the franchise for the next 86 years. In Ruth's first three full seasons in Boston, he went 65–33 as a starting pitcher. But teammate Harry Hooper could not help noticing Ruth's hitting prowess, too, and in 1918 Ruth played in the outfield for 59 games, making just 19 starts as a pitcher—half his total from the previous year. Ruth did start twice in the World Series, winning both decisions to make him 3-0 with a 0.87 ERA in World Series play, but his offensive prowess was becoming his calling card. In 1919, Ruth played 111 games in the outfield and set a new home run record, with 29. He also demanded a raise, and owner Harry Frazee, a New Yorker who financed Broadway plays, responded by selling him to the Yankees. Baseball was never the same.

JOE CRONIN

When owner Tom Yawkey paid $250,000 to the Washington Senators in Oct. 1934 for Joe Cronin, he knew what he was getting: a champion manager who was also among the most productive hitters in the game. Cronin, a shortstop, had driven in 100 runs in five consecutive seasons for the Senators and had guided them to the World Series as a 26-year-old rookie manager in 1933. He played his last 11 seasons with Boston, batting .300 in his Red Sox career and managing the team through 1947, a span that included the 1946 pennant. Cronin stayed on as Red Sox general manager through 1958, but part of his legacy is that the Sox did not field a single black player during his tenure. The first, Pumpsie Green, joined thc team in 1959, after Cronin had taken a job as the American League president, a position he would hold until 1973.

LEFTY GROVE

Lefty Grove was 34 years old when he first pitched for the Red Sox in 1934, after the Philadelphia A's sold him for $125,000 and two players. Grove was the best pitcher of his era, compiling exactly 300 victories and doing it all after the Dead Ball era. Grove's success in the lively-ball era has led some historians to consider him the best pitcher in history; indeed, Grove was the only pitcher to win his 300th game between 1924 and 1961. He never had a losing season in eight years with the Red Sox, winning 20 games in 1935 and going 29–8 over the '38 and '39 seasons. Grove's .680 winning percentage is the highest among 300-game winners.

JIMMIE FOXX

The Red Sox, who had experience in selling
star players, became buyers in the 1930s
when the Depression caused Connie Mack to
break up his Philadelphia A's. Two years after
purchasing Lefty Grove for $125,000 and two
players, the Red Sox bought Jimmie Foxx—also
known, appropriately, as "The Beast"—for
$150,000 and two players. Foxx would spend
six extremely productive seasons in Boston,
winning the MVP award in 1938 with a .349
average, 50 homers and 175 runs batted in.
The home run and RBI totals are still club
records. Not surprisingly, Foxx set the major
league record for walks in a game that season,
with six. The Red Sox would finish in second
place three times during Foxx's years, but
they did not win a pennant with him.

BOBBY DOERR

When Bobby Doerr retired because of back pain at age 33, in 1951, nobody had played more games in a Red Sox uniform than his 1,865. Doerr served with distinction as the Sox second baseman from 1937 to '51, finally joining the Hall of Fame in 1986. Doerr ranked in the top 10 in the AL in extra-base hits nine times in a 10-year span, and had a lifetime average of .288. That was augmented by his spectacular success at Fenway Park, where Doerr hit .315, compared to .256 on the road. He batted .409 in the Red Sox' 1946 World Series loss to the Cardinals.

TED WILLIAMS

Officially, the MVP of the 1999 All-Star Game was Pedro Martinez. But to anyone who was there, the night belonged to Ted Williams. In a pre-game ceremony, Williams was back on his old Fenway green, surrounded by modern All-Stars all but genuflecting at his golf cart. The spine-tingling scene was a testament to the aura and majesty of Williams, who probably attained his goal of being the greatest hitter who ever lived. Williams, known alternately as "the Kid," "Teddy Ballgame," "the Splendid Splinter" and "the Thumper," was the last man to bat .400, hitting .406 in 1941. He won the Triple Crown in 1942 and 1947 and belted a homer in his final at-bat on Sept. 28, 1960. He hit .344 over 19 seasons, and his career .482 on-base percentage is the highest in major league history. Williams could be ornery or charming, but he was always fiercely proud and competitive. A scientist of hitting who was said to have 20/10 vision, Williams had a walk-to-strikeout ratio of roughly 3 to 1. He lost nearly five prime seasons to military service in the Navy Air Corps during World War II and on a Marine fighter jet in the Korean War, but still belted 521 career homers. When Williams died, in 2002, his teammate and friend Bobby Doerr said the words Williams always wanted to hear: "I think he was the best hitter that baseball has had."

CARL YASTRZEMSKI

No man in history has played more games for one team than the 3,308 Carl Yastrzemski played for the Red Sox from 1961 through 1983. Yastrzemski, who played shortstop for Notre Dame, replaced the venerable Ted Williams in left field and upheld Williams' legacy. In 1967, Yastrzemski enjoyed one of the best seasons ever, batting .326 with 44 homers and 121 runs batted in, becoming the last player to capture the Triple Crown. He added his third batting title the next year, at .301 (the year before baseball lowered the mound), and finished with 3,419 hits, sixth on the career list. Though Yaz made the last out of the 1975 World Series and the one-game playoff with the Yankees in 1978, he was generally outstanding in the clutch, with a .369 average in three postseason series.

CARLTON FISK

In Boston lore, Carlton "Pudge" Fisk will forever be 27 years old, wearing No. 27, waving his arms desperately to his right as his home run crashes into the foul pole to win Game 6 of the 1975 World Series. Born in Vermont and raised in Charlestown, N.H., Fisk was destined to be a hero in New England. He won the AL Rookie of the Year award in 1972 and played for Boston through 1980. His fierce work ethic enabled him to set a record for games caught, 2,226, and though he played longer for the Chicago White Sox, Fisk entered the Hall of Fame with a Red Sox cap in 2000.

DENNIS ECKERSLEY

A few days before the fateful 1978 season, the Red Sox traded four players to the Indians for Dennis Eckersley. Twenty years later, in 1998, Eckersley threw his final major league pitch in a Boston uniform. Alas, it was in a second tour with the Red Sox, who traded Eckersley to the Cubs in 1984 for none other than Bill Buckner. Eckersley was a starter for the Sox from '78 to '84, winning 20 games in his first Boston season and going 84–70 overall. Converted to the bullpen by the A's in 1987, Eckersley became the most dominant reliever of his era. When Oakland swept the Red Sox in the 1988 and 1990 ALCS, Eckersley saved six of the seven games. But it was the fact that he had been a dominant starter in Boston that cinched his selection to Cooperstown.

WADE BOGGS

When Wade Boggs reached the Hall of Fame in 2005, he reflected often on the perseverance it took even to get to the major leagues, let alone compile 3,010 hits. A seventh-round draft pick by the Red Sox in 1976, Boggs languished in the minors for six years. The last of those seasons, 1981, he led the International League in hitting and was not even called up in September. Boggs had little speed and was said to have just one skill, hitting for average. But when finally given the chance in 1982, he showed he could do that better than just about anyone. Boggs, who said he ate chicken before every game and followed many other superstitions, batted .349 in '82 and captured the first of five batting titles the next year. He also had a .400 on-base percentage 11 times, including twice with the Yankees. But Boggs' glory days were in Boston, where he helped the Red Sox to the 1986 World Series and two other division titles.

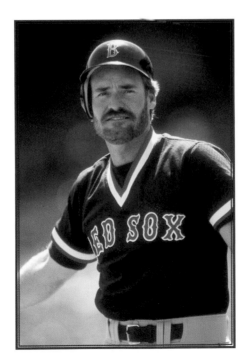

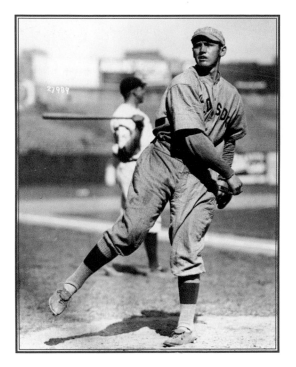

Other Red Sox Greats

SMOKEY JOE WOOD

The hardest thrower of his era, "Smokey Joe" Wood got his nickname from his sizzling fastball. He pitched eight seasons for the Red Sox, winning 23 games in 1919 and tossing a no-hitter. In 1912, Wood posted a remarkable 34–5 record, capping it with three victories in Boston's World Series triumph over the Giants. After going 15–5 for the 1915 champs, Wood was overcome by a shoulder injury and essentially gave up pitching. He continued his career for five more years as an outfielder for the Cleveland Indians, helping them win the 1920 World Series. Wood, who lived to be 95 years old, later spent 20 years as the head baseball coach at Yale.

DOM DIMAGGIO

The brother of the Yankees' Hall of Fame center fielder, the bespectacled Dominic DiMaggio was a standout in his own right, making seven All-Star teams in 10 full major league seasons. DiMaggio played his whole career with the Red Sox, missing three years due to Navy service in World War II. In his first year back, 1946, the Red Sox won their only pennant in the span from 1919 through 1966. Ever approachable and a lifelong friend to Ted Williams, DiMaggio's personality contrasted with that of his brother Joe. But the brothers shared hitting streaks in common; Joe holds the major league record, at 56, and Dominic's 34-game streak in 1949 is the longest in Red Sox history.

JOHNNY PESKY

Baseball uniforms have always suited Johnny Pesky. When he first got into the game, he was washing them as a clubhouse boy for the Pacific Coast League's Portland Beavers. Well into his 80s, he was still wearing one as a special assignment instructor for the Red Sox. Pesky joined the Sox in 1942, batting .331 with 205 hits. He lost the next three years to his service in World War II, but came back with 200-hit seasons in '46 and '47. Pesky was the perfect name for a player who once drew 100 walks in a season while striking out just 19 times. A career .307 hitter, Pesky's legacy might have been defined by allegedly holding a relay throw a split-second too long in Game 7 of the 1946 World Series, when Enos Slaughter dashed home to score the winning run for St. Louis. Instead, Pesky's lively personality and boundless enthusiasm have made him beloved, not reviled, to generations of Red Sox fans.

LUIS TIANT

It was said that Luis Tiant's eyes darted to every fan in the stands at least once a game because of his whirling, frenetic delivery. That was just part of the fun of watching Tiant, the son of a star Cuban pitcher who once struck out Babe Ruth in an exhibition. In the 1970s, Tiant was the ace of the Red Sox rotation, and they got him for nothing. A 21-game winner with a 1.60 ERA for Cleveland in 1968, Tiant succumbed to a shoulder injury and was released by the Atlanta Braves in 1971 without pitching for the team. Salvaged by the Red Sox, Tiant struggled that season but won 15 games in '72 as the Sox finished a half-game behind the division-winning Tigers. He won 20 or more games in three of the next four seasons and beat the Reds twice in the 1975 World Series. Tiant pitched in Boston through 1978, and many years later his thick Fu Manchu mustache is still seen regularly around the Red Sox, for whom he works as a special instructor.

DWIGHT EVANS

Dwight Evans had played about 400 games for the Red Sox before the 1975 postseason, so people knew who he was. Still, it took a breathtaking play in the World Series to establish Evans as a defensive star. A master of the crannies in right field at Fenway, Evans robbed Joe Morgan of an extra-base hit that would have put the Reds ahead in the eleventh inning of the famous Game 6. Not surprisingly, the play earned exposure for Evans that resulted, in 1976, in the first of eight Gold Gloves. Second only to Carl Yastrzemski in games played for the Red Sox, with 2,505, Evans led the team in RBIs in the 1986 World Series, with nine.

JIM RICE

The most feared American League slugger of his era was Jim Ed Rice, an eight-time All-Star who led the league in total bases four times from 1977 to 1983. Rice played his entire 16-year career with the Red Sox, retiring after the 1989 season with 382 home runs, trailing only Ted Williams and Carl Yastrzemski on the Sox' career list. Rice won the Most Valuable Player award in 1978, when he hit .315 with 46 homers and 139 runs batted in as the Red Sox lost a one-game AL East playoff to the Yankees. Possessing enormous strength—he once broke his bat on a check-swing, without hitting the ball—Rice missed the 1975 World Series with a broken left hand. He hit .333 against the Mets in the '86 Series, but did not drive in a run.

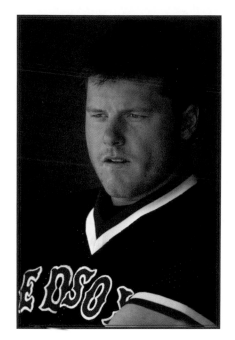

ROGER CLEMENS

When the cab driver first dropped him off at Fenway Park, Roger Clemens, the long, tall Texan drafted in the first round by the Red Sox in 1983, thought there was a mistake. Used to wide open spaces, Clemens wanted to know where the ballpark was. Though unfamiliar with the tight confines of Kenmore Square, Clemens quickly learned how to manage. After shoulder surgery in 1985, his second season, he came back in 1986 with a remarkable 24–4 showing that earned him the Cy Young, the MVP award and a trip to the World Series. Clemens became the first pitcher to record 20 strikeouts in a nine-inning game that season, a feat he repeated in his final month with the Red Sox in 1996. Though Clemens led the AL in strikeouts in '96, GM Dan Duquette believed he was in the "twilight of his career," and let him sign with Toronto as a free agent. It was a gross misjudgment, and most observers believe Clemens used the comment as motivation for the rest of his career. Through 2005, he had 341 career victories, including 192 with the Red Sox, tied with Cy Young for most in franchise history.

NOMAR GARCIAPARRA

By the time of his trade to the Cubs on July 31, 2004, Nomar Garciaparra seemed distanced from the scruffy group that would capture the Red Sox' first title in 86 years. But for the seven years before that, the Red Sox were Nomar's team. He splashed onto the Fenway stage as the 1997 Rookie of the Year, rapping 85 extra-base hits and driving in 98 runs. He would go on to win two batting titles (1999 and 2000) and make five All-Star teams, and his average in five postseason series was .323. His singular highlight came on May 10, 1999, against Seattle, when he tied the club single-game record for home runs and runs batted in, blasting three homers, including two grand slams, and driving in 10.

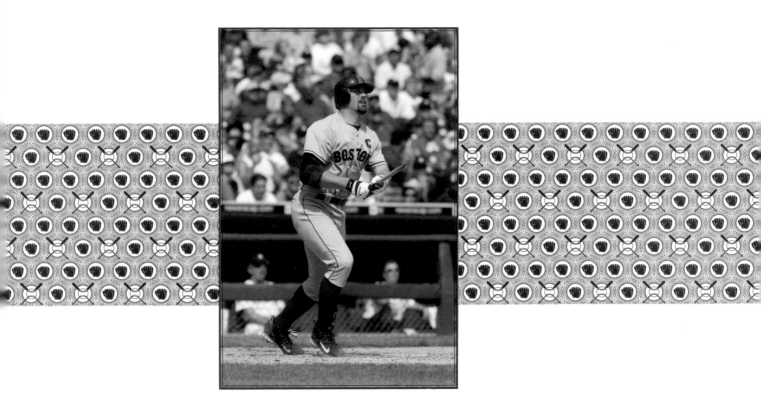

JASON VARITEK

At the July trading deadline in 1997, the Red Sox were prepared to trade reliever Heathcliff
Slocumb to the Seattle Mariners for pitcher Derek Lowe or catcher Jason Varitek. As the story
goes, the desperate Mariners believed the Red Sox wanted both players, not just one, and gave
in. It became one of the most lopsided trades in history, eventually helping the Red Sox win
the World Series. Deeply respected in the clubhouse for his honesty, preparation and handling
of pitchers, Varitek was named the team captain upon signing a four-year, $40 million contract
extension after the 2004 season. He is only the third Sox captain since World War II, following
Carl Yastrzemski and Jim Rice.

PEDRO MARTINEZ

While Dan Duquette blundered by failing to re-sign Roger Clemens after the 1996 season, no one doubted that he found a suitable replacement. Duquette watched from afar in '97 as Pedro Martinez, just 25 years old, won a Cy Young Award for the small-market Expos. He was determined to trade for Martinez and did so after the season, shipping pitching prospects Carl Pavano and Tony Armas Jr. to Montreal and then quickly signing Martinez to a contract that would keep him in Boston through 2004. Demonstrative on the mound and mysterious off it, Martinez became a happening at Fenway, and he fed off the frenzied fans. He captured two Cy Young awards for the Red Sox, in 1999 and 2000, punctuating the '99 season by winning the All-Star Game MVP award at Fenway Park and dominating the Indians and Yankees in the postseason. In his final start for Boston, he worked seven shutout innings in St. Louis to win Game 3 of the 2004 World Series. Martinez left for the Mets that winter with a 117–37 record in his Red Sox career, giving him a .760 winning percentage that ranks as the best in team history.

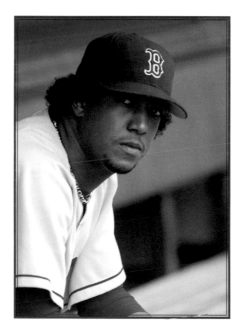

MANNY RAMIREZ

Signed for eight years and $160 million after the 2000 season by General Manager Dan Duquette, Ramirez took aim at the Green Monster with his effortless swing. The Monster hardly stood a chance. Already a megastar with the Indians, Ramirez remained an overwhelming offensive force at Fenway Park. He topped 30 homers and 100 RBIs in each of his first five seasons with the Red Sox, often dodging trade rumors, and sometimes encouraging them. Ramirez came off as flaky and spacey, and the Sox nearly dealt him to Texas for Alex Rodriguez in late 2003. The trade never materialized, and Ramirez retuned to Fenway, winning the Most Valuable Player award in the World Series by batting .412 with a homer in the sweep of the Cardinals.giving him a .760 winning percentage that ranks as the best in team history.

Doug Mientkiewicz, Keith Foulke and Jason Varitek of the Boston Red Sox celebrate after defeating the St. Louis Cardinals 3-0 in game four of the World Series on October 27, 2004 at Busch Stadium in St. Louis.

THE GREAT TEAMS

Contrary to popular belief, the pride and unity of Red Sox Nation has been built not on the shared experience of losing but rather on watching team after team aim for greatness. Most fell just short, but we start with the team that exorcised the demons and reversed the Curse, once and for all.

———— 2004 ————

On Oct. 27, 2004, a fan sitting at the top of Busch Stadium in right field could look to the field below and make a startling discovery. In the ninth inning of Game 4 of the World Series, the Red Sox right fielder, Gabe Kapler, wore No. 19. The center fielder, Johnny Damon, wore No. 18. With their backs to the stands, the numbers in a fan's line of vision were 19 and 18.

Nineteen eighteen. How many times had the Red Sox heard that chant? How many times had they been taunted, usually by Yankee fans, for not winning a title since 1918? How many times had they cursed The Curse, that mythical force hanging over their every move? How many times had they wished that their forefathers, just once in the last 86 years, had managed to win a world championship?

It had never happened, they all knew—not since the Sox sold Babe Ruth to the Yankees in 1920. Since then, the Yankees had 26 championships and the Red Sox none, coming close several times but losing in excruciating fashion.

The first World Series loss had been in St. Louis, the very city where they would stomp out their ghosts for good in 2004. Seven-game defeats in four World Series—1946, 1967, 1975 and 1986—and other spectacular failures had infused fans with a sense of dread.

But there was also hope. Always, there was hope. How else to explain the phenomenon the Red Sox had become by 2004? They have always mattered greatly to the psyche of New England, but in 2004 it was different.

The playoff loss in 2003 had been crushing. The Red Sox had a three-run lead with one out in the eighth inning of Game 7 of the American League Championship Series at Yankee Stadium, only to lose on Aaron Boone's home run in the eleventh. But the fans still believed. For the first time in franchise history, the Red Sox sold every available seat in a season. Eighty-one home games in 2004, 81 sellouts.

The winter had brought the promise of better things. The Sox' grand plans for the offense—replacing Manny Ramirez and Nomar Garciaparra with Alex Rodriguez and Magglio Ordonez—never materialized, but they added an ace starter, Curt Schilling, and a top closer, Keith Foulke.

Schilling came to Boston in a trade with the Arizona Diamondbacks, but he had to approve the deal. General manager Theo Epstein had Thanksgiving dinner at Schilling's home near Phoenix, and Schilling, acting as his own agent, made it clear he understood what was expected of him. He asked for and received a clause in his contract that would pay him a $2 million bonus if the Red Sox won the World Series in 2004,

After a hot start, though, the Red Sox went 40–39 from May 1 through July 30. The next day was the trading deadline, and Epstein decided the Red Sox could not win the World Series without a shakeup.

So he engineered a four-way trade that shipped longtime shortstop Nomar Garciaparra to the Cubs and brought back a better defensive shortstop, Orlando Cabrera, plus a defensive specialist for first base, Doug Mientkiewicz. Epstein also made a subtle

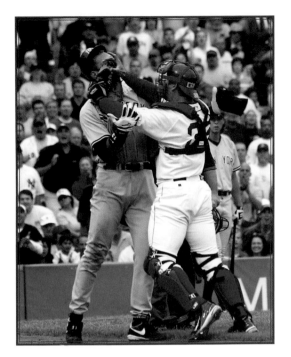

move, acquiring outfielder Dave Roberts in a trade with the Los Angeles Dodgers.

There had already been rumblings of an on-field awakening, starting with a July 24 thriller against the Yankees at Fenway Park. The game had ended with Bill Mueller's walk-off homer against Mariano Rivera, but the lasting image came earlier, when catcher Jason Varitek shoved his glove in Rodriguez's face, inciting a brawl.

Whether the fight sparked the Red Sox, who called themselves "idiots" and thrived on a rowdy image, was debatable. There was no doubt about the impact of the trades. With tighter defense and a deeper bench—and an offense few teams could contain—the Red Sox sprinted to a 42–18 finish, easily winning the AL wild card for the second year in a row.

The Red Sox swept the Angels in three games in the division series, winning the clincher on a homer over The Wall by David Ortiz (aka Big Papi), who hit .545 for the series. The Yankees had also won their division series, setting up a rematch in the ALCS.

David Ortiz

On the eve of Game 1 at Yankee Stadium, Schilling joked in the interview room that he could think of nothing better than making 55,000 New York fans shut up. There was little talk of his ankle injury, which he had aggravated in his division series start in Anaheim.

"The only thing it affects is the drive off the rubber," Schilling said, adding, "I'm not planning on it being an issue."

Those words were more foreboding than they seemed at the time. Driving off the rubber is the foundation for every pitcher; without proper drive, everything is affected. Sure enough, in Game 1, the Yankees clobbered Schilling for six runs in three innings of a 10–7 victory. The next day, the Red Sox announced that Schilling was doubtful for the rest of the postseason.

The sheath that housed a tendon in Schilling's right ankle was torn, causing the tendon to snap in and out of position when he pitched. The custom ankle brace Schilling had tried for Game 1 had failed.

The Red Sox followed that announcement by losing Game 2. Pedro Martinez, whose frustration with the Yankees in September had led to an infamous remark—"I just tip my hat and call the Yankees my daddy"—lost to Jon Lieber, 3–1. After a rain-out and an off-day, the Yankees punished the Sox in Game 3 at Fenway Park, 19–8.

The gloom over Boston was palpable. On the morning of Game 4, the First Baptist Church near Fenway offered this topic for Sunday worship: "Why Does God Allow Suffering?" It seemed like a painfully appropriate sermon for Red Sox Nation.

In the ninth inning that night, the Red Sox truly seemed to have no prayer. They were facing Rivera, the greatest closer in postseason history, the MVP of the ALCS the year before. They were losing by a run, three outs from a sweep.

But Kevin Millar led off with a walk, and Epstein's July 31 trade paid off in a big way. Roberts ran for Millar and had one thought in mind: steal second base. When he noticed third-base coach Dale Sveum giving the bunt sign to Mueller, he called time and told first-base coach Lynn Jones that he wanted to run.

Sveum took the sign off. Roberts broke for second, sliding headfirst to beat Derek Jeter's tag. Then Mueller rapped a single through the middle, scoring Roberts with the tying run.

The Red Sox won in 12 innings on another

walk-off homer by Ortiz, but they were still attempting to do something never done in baseball history. No team that had fallen behind by 3–0 in a postseason series had even forced a Game 7, let alone won the series. And when the Yankees took a 4–2 lead into the eighth inning of Game 5, the Red Sox were on the brink again.

But again, Ortiz delivered. He led off the eighth with a homer, and pinch-runner Roberts again scored the tying run, this time on a sacrifice fly. The Sox bullpen shut out the Yankees for the last eight innings of the game—veteran knuckle-baller Tim Wakefield worked the final three and Ortiz won it in 14 with a single.

The momentum had swung to Boston's side, especially with Schilling back on the mound for Game 6. The team doctor, Bill Morgan, had devised a temporary fix for the ankle, suturing the skin around the tendon to the deep tissue. The reconstructed sheath would keep

the tendon from snapping over the bone, and Schilling—with blood seeping through his white sock—held the Yankees to one run over seven innings in a 4–1 victory. Even Rodriguez's infamous slap play on the bases against reliever Bronson Arroyo could not help the Yankees.

Game 7 was a 10–3 mauling, with the Yankees scraping just one hit in six innings off Derek Lowe, who was working on two days' rest. Damon belted two homers, including a grand slam in the second inning, and Ortiz finished with a .387 average to win the MVP award for the series.

"There's no curse," said catcher Jason Varitek, drenched in champagne that night. "The curse, in my opinion, was just being outplayed. That team outplayed us over the years."

The Red Sox had finally trumped the Yankees, but they still needed to vanquish the Cardinals to fully squash Ruth's curse. That

★★★★★★★★★★★★★★★★★★★★★★★★

would prove to be remarkably easy.

The linescores alone showed that something had changed in the cosmos. The Red Sox made four errors in Game 1 at Fenway Park, and four more in Game 2. Yet they won both games.

Mark Bellhorn's eighth-inning homer lifted them to an 11–9 victory in Game 1, as Foulke earned the victory with clutch relief work. Six gritty innings by Schilling—bloody sock and all—gave the Sox a 6–2 victory the next night.

The Cardinals, meanwhile, were struggling to throw a pitch past the Red Sox. The St. Louis starters threw 369 pitches in the World Series, and the Red Sox swung and missed just 16 times. Boston scored in the first inning of all four games and did not trail at any point in any game.

Ramirez homered in the first inning of Game 3 at St. Louis, and he threw out a runner at the plate in the bottom of the inning, atoning for his two errors in Game 1. Martinez—making his final Boston start—fired seven shutout innings for the victory, allowing three hits.

Lowe had the same results the next night, and Damon's leadoff homer gave the Red Sox the only run they would need. They led 3–0 in the ninth inning, with Foulke on to face the fearsome Albert Pujols, Scott Rolen and Jim Edmonds.

Pujols singled, but Rolen had no hits in the series, and Edmonds had a lonely bunt single in Game 1. Rolen flied out. Edmonds fanned. Up stepped Edgar Renteria, wearing No. 3: Ruth's number for the Yankees.

Derek Lowe and Jason Varitek, 2004

Foulke surely did not notice, or care. He speared Renteria's comebacker, took a few steps to first and carefully tossed the ball underhanded to Mientkiewicz for the final out. Varitek leaped into Foulke's arms, and the Red Sox were free.

They were free of Ruth's curse, free of the angst and foreboding in the stands. They had changed history over eight glorious games, rewarding and redeeming the most loyal fans in baseball.

"This is bigger than the 25 guys in this clubhouse," said Epstein, the Brookline native who raised the trophy in the winners' clubhouse. "This is for all of Red Sox Nation, past and present."

Other Great Teams

1903

They were known as the Boston Pilgrims of the American League, and their matchup with the National League's Pittsburgh Pirates in the first "world's championship series" was no accident. The owners, Henry Killilea of Boston and Barney Dreyfus of Pittsburgh, had made a bold deal in August, arranging for their first-place teams to stage a best-of-nine postseason series. The teams indeed won their respective major leagues, setting up the first interleague meeting. Cy Young gave up four runs in the top of the first inning of Game 1, and the Pirates won three of the first four games. But the Pilgrims came back to take the last four and the title, with Young winning twice. Bill Dinneen went 3–1 for the Pilgrims, winning the finale at Huntington Avenue Grounds in Boston by the score of 3–0. That would be the same score in the last game of the 100th World Series, in 2004, when the Red Sox—the modern-day Pilgrims—took home the title in St. Louis.

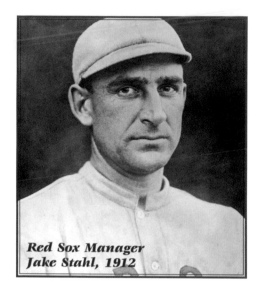

*Red Sox Manager
Jake Stahl, 1912*

1912

A banner year in Red Sox history was 1912, when Fenway Park opened and the Red Sox won their second championship. First baseman Jake Stahl debuted as manager and led the Red Sox to a 105–47 record, their best ever. Smokey Joe Wood led the staff with 34 victories, while Tris Speaker collected 222 hits, a career high. In the World Series, the Red Sox capitalized on an error years before they would make heartbreak their specialty. In Game 8 against the Giants (the second game had ended in a tie), the Sox trailed by 2–1 entering the bottom of the 10th at Fenway. Pinch hitter Clyde Engle led off with a routine fly to center field that Fred Snodgrass dropped for an error. "Snodgrass' Muff," as it became known, gave the Sox the opening they needed. A one-out single by Speaker—whose foul ball had dropped safely near first base—tied the game, and the Red Sox won the title on a sacrifice fly by Larry Gardner, beating the great Christy Mathewson.

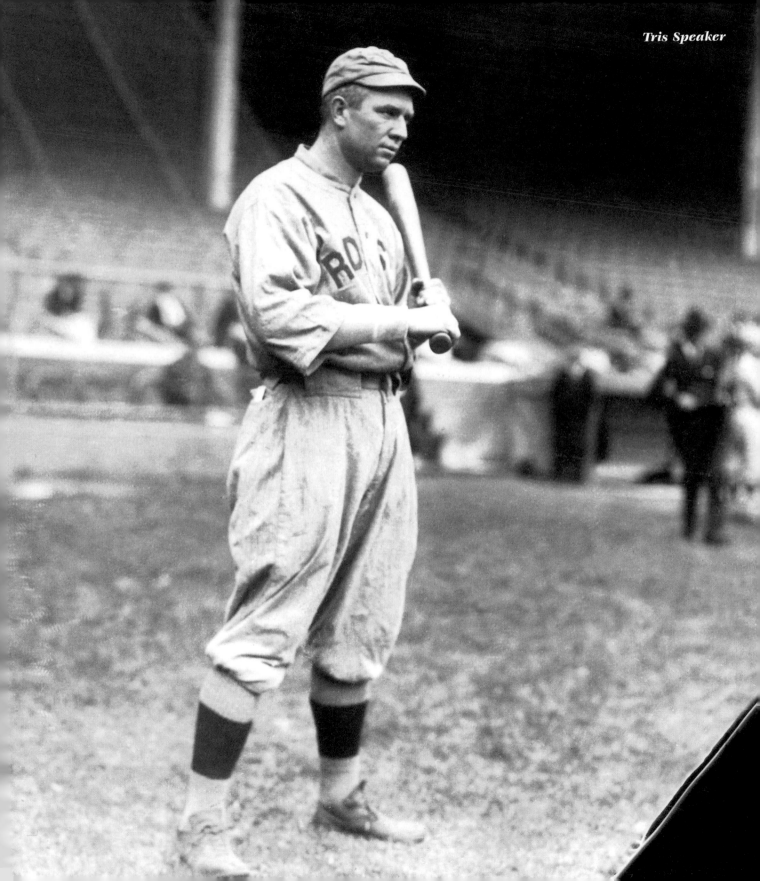

Tris Speaker

Babe Ruth

Ruth, pitcher

BOSTON RED SOX READY FOR WORLD'S-SERIES BATTLE

1915

A year after the "Miracle Braves" rose from last place in July to champions in October, the Red Sox kept the title in Boston with a victory over the Philadelphia Phillies in the World Series. Babe Ruth had made his debut the year before, and this was his first full season. His ledger included an 18–8 record as a pitcher and four homers in 92 at-bats at the plate. He made only a cameo appearance in the World Series, grounding out to first as a pinch-hitter in the Red Sox' Game 1 loss. The Sox won the next four, as Rube Foster, Dutch Leonard, Ernie Shore and Foster again tossed complete games. The Sox came back to win the fifth and final game at Philadelphia's Baker Bowl after trailing 4–2 in the eighth. They tied it that inning on a two-run homer by Duffy Lewis, and scored the Series-winning run when Harry Hooper homered off Eppa Rixey in the top of the ninth.

Harry Hooper steps on home plate after hitting the winning home run in the 1915 World Series in Philadelphia.

1916

Manager Bill Carrigan, the Lewiston, Maine, native and the Red Sox' reserve catcher, guided the Sox to back-to-back championships for the only time in team history. They did it without Tris Speaker, who was shipped to Cleveland for two players and $55,000 after a contract dispute, and Smokey Joe Wood, a contract holdout whose pitching career had been ruined by injuries. Babe Ruth emerged as the big winner in the rotation with a 23–12 record, and Carl Mays won 18 after pitching in relief the year before. Ruth worked all 14 innings in Game 2 of the World Series to beat Brooklyn, and Ernie Shore won twice, including a three-hitter in Game 5 to clinch the title.

1918

They did not know it at the time, of course, but the 1918 Red Sox would be the last Boston team to win the World Series in the 20th century. They did it in a shortened season against the backdrop of World War I, with the Series played from Sept. 5 through Sept. 11 because of wartime restrictions. The Red Sox had lost Duffy Lewis and others to military service, but their pitchers had a 2.31 ERA, second-best in the league. Sam Jones, who had been 4–11 in his career, went 16–5. Carl Mays won 21 games. And the great Babe Ruth went 13–7 while spending most of his time in the outfield. Ruth batted .300 and won his first home run title, with 11. In the World Series against the Cubs, Ruth and Mays combined to go 4–0 with a 1.03 earned run average. Mays won the clincher in Game 6 with a three-hit complete game before just 15,238 fans at Fenway.

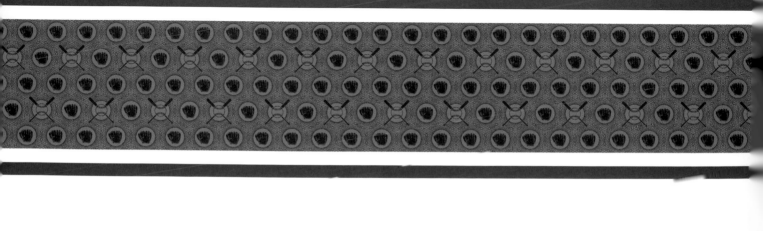

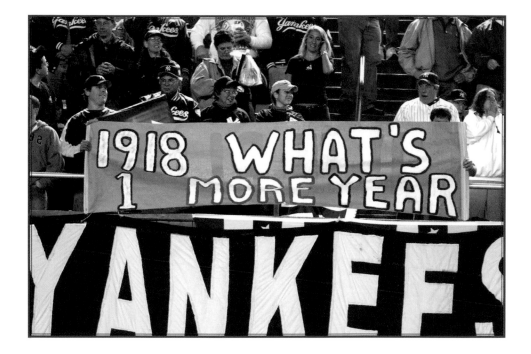

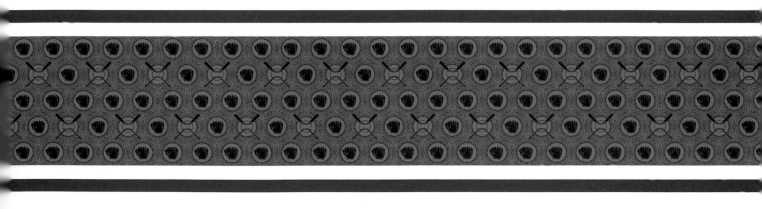

1946

When the Red Sox' stars returned after World War II, they believed they were on the verge of becoming a dynasty. They had finished in second place four times in five years before the war. In 1946, they had two 20-game winners, Tex Hughson and Boo Ferris, and a slugging first baseman, Rudy York, to go with the core of Ted Williams, Bobby Doerr, Johnny Pesky and Dominic DiMaggio. It added up to a 104–50 regular-season record and an easy AL pennant. In the National League, the Cardinals and the Dodgers needed a two-game playoff to determine who would play Boston. While they waited, the Red Sox tried to stay sharp with an exhibition game against AL stars. It was then that Williams was hit on the right elbow with a pitch, and he would bat just .200 (5 for 25) against St. Louis in the Series. Still, the Red Sox had chances to win. They led the series, 3–2, before losing Games 6 and 7 in St. Louis. Enos Slaughter scored the winning run in the eighth inning of Game 7, charging home from first base on a two-out double by Dixie Walker. Pesky has been blamed for hesitating on his throw home, but there is little hard evidence that he did. The truth was that Slaughter ran on the arm of Leon Culberson, the center fielder who had come in after DiMaggio twisted his ankle on his game-tying double in the top of the inning. Culberson's lob gave Pesky no time to catch Slaughter, and the Red Sox went down in seven. The same group of players never made it back to the Series, as Hughson and Ferris quickly succumbed to injuries and the Yankees resumed their stranglehold on the American League.

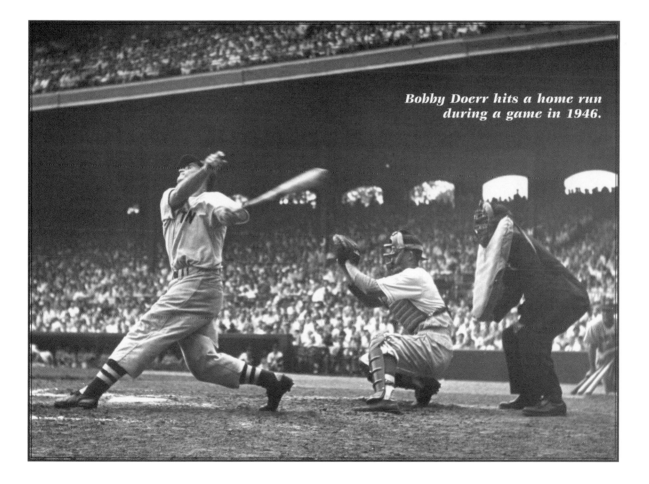

Bobby Doerr hits a home run during a game in 1946.

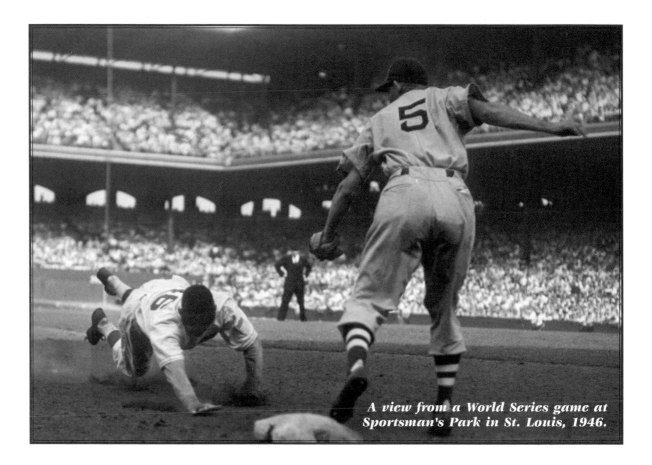

A view from a World Series game at Sportsman's Park in St. Louis, 1946.

Rudy York crosses home plate after hitting the winning home run in the tenth inning of the first game of the 1946 World Series in St. Louis.

Jim Lonborg, 1967

1967

The Red Sox had finished below .500 for eight consecutive seasons and had captured just one pennant in the last 49 years. They had a rookie manager, Dick Williams, no clear ace in the rotation, and a left fielder named Carl Yastrzemski who had never hit more than 20 home runs. But so much changed that summer of the Impossible Dream. Yastrzemski won the Triple Crown. Jim Lonborg, 19–27 in his career, rose up to go 22–9. Shortstop Rico Petrocelli came into his own and outfielder Reggie Smith burst onto the scene. There was tragedy, too; young slugger Tony Conigliaro was hit in the eye by a Jack Hamilton pitch

that August, all but ruining a promising career. But the Red Sox carried on, outlasting the Tigers, Twins and White Sox for the pennant. Lonborg spun a one-hit shutout in Game 2 of the World Series against the Cardinals at Fenway, but the Sox lost three of the first four games before rallying to win Games 5 and 6 and set up a finale at home. Lonborg took the ball on two days' rest, and his opponent, Bob Gibson, had three. Both had two victories in the Series, but it was Gibson who would get a third. He worked his third complete game of the series, allowing just three hits and slamming a homer in the Cardinals' 7–2 victory.

Jim Lonborg, 1967

Luis Tiant pitches against the Cincinnati Reds during the World Series at Fenway Park in 1975.

1975

Eight years after the Impossible Dream, Carl Yastrzemski and Rico Petrocelli remained to lead a new generation of Red Sox heroes. With the colorful Luis Tiant and Bill Lee headlining the rotation and an all-under-24 outfield of Jim Rice, Fred Lynn and Dwight Evans, the Sox captured the division and swept three-time champion Oakland to win the pennant. Lynn became the first man to win MVP and Rookie of the Year honors in the same season, but Rice missed the postseason with a broken wrist. Still, the Red Sox nearly won without him. Their classic seven-game World Series with the Cincinnati Reds brought many fans back to baseball, and featured perhaps the

most memorable clip in televised sports history, the shot of Carlton Fisk willing fair his winning homer in Game 6. As they would in 1986, the Red Sox led Game 7 by 3–0 in the sixth inning. But Tony Perez bashed Lee's "Leephus" pitch that inning for a two-run homer, and the Reds tied the game off Roger Moret in the seventh. After $1\frac{1}{3}$ shutout innings by Jim Willoughby, manager Darrell Johnson chose a rookie, Jim Burton, to pitch the ninth inning. Two walks and a two-out single by Joe Morgan brought in the Series-winning run. Burton would pitch only one more game in the major leagues, and the Red Sox would endure 29 more years of torture.

1986

The 1986 Red Sox had everything but a proven closer. They had Roger Clemens going 24–4 at the front of the rotation, supported by a tough lefty, Bruce Hurst, and a passionate 16-game winner, Oil Can Boyd. They had ample power—Jim Rice, Dwight Evans, Don Baylor—and the batting champion in Wade Boggs. They had grit, winning the ALCS in seven games after being one strike from elimination in Game 5 against the Angels. But they did not have that steely-eyed closer, and that is what cost them the World Series. Dave Henderson, the hero of the ALCS, had homered in the top of the 10th inning of Game 6 against the Mets at Shea Stadium, and the Red Sox looked to Calvin Schiraldi to close down the Series. With two outs and no base runners, Schiraldi gave up three successive singles as the Mets closed within one. Bob Stanley, the club's career leader in games pitched, came in to face Mookie Wilson. Red Sox fans know the rest: two-strike wild pitch past catcher Rich Gedman, tie game. Error by Buckner, Mets win. Schiraldi lost Game 7, too, allowing Ray Knight's tie-breaking homer in the seventh inning. Boggs cried on the bench after Marty Barrett struck out to end the Series, and all of New England wept with him.

Wade Boggs watches the flight of the ball as he follows through on his swing during a game in the 1986 World Series against the New York Mets at Shea Stadium.

Dave Henderson, World Series 1986

Roger Clemens, World Series 1986

—————— So Close ——————

The history of the Boston Red Sox is defined in many ways by heartbreak, by the wafer-thin difference between victory and defeat, agony and ecstasy. Rather than ignore the heartbreak, we chronicle here some of those memorable near-misses that combined to make the 2004 season so cathartic for Red Sox Nation.

1948-49

Denny Galehouse. The name still sticks in the psyche of Red Sox fans. Two years after winning the pennant in '46, Ted Williams & Co. had another shot at the Series, and manager Joe McCarthy put the season in the hands of ... Galehouse? Spurning ace Mel Parnell, who had three days' rest, for the element of surprise in Galehouse, McCarthy saw his decision backfire. Cleveland player-manager Lou Boudreau had four hits, including two homers, in an 8–3 victory by the Tribe. Galehouse, who never had another decision in the majors, allowed a three-run homer to Ken Keltner that broke a 1–1 tie in the fourth inning. The next season brought another failure on the last day of the season. Needing to win one of two games at Yankee Stadium to capture the pennant, the Red Sox lost both. They had their best pitchers on the mound this time—Parnell in the first game, Ellis Kinder in the second—but the Yankees won both, ending the '40s on a discouraging note for the Sox. It would be worse in the '50s, when the Red Sox did not win a single pennant.

1978

There are certain seasons that scar a fan base for years; just ask any Phillies fan about 1964. For Red Sox Nation, that season was 1978. When former Yankee Mike Torrez beat the Brewers on July 19, the Red Sox were 62–28, nine games up on Milwaukee in the AL East and 14 games ahead of the fourth-place Yankees. When the Sox lost nine of their next 10, the lead was cut in half, and the Yankees were stalking, just eight back. It didn't matter that Jim Rice was having an MVP season, the first AL player with 400 total bases since Joe DiMaggio in 1937. The Yankees were charging, and they burst into a first-place tie with the four-game "Boston Massacre" at Fenway in early September, sweeping the series by a combined score of 42–9. The Red Sox would win 12 of 14 to finish in a tie with the Yankees after 162 games, but Bucky Dent came to town for a one-game playoff on Oct. 2 ... and Sox fans know the rest.

2003

With star power and bargain-priced additions tailored for Fenway Park, the 2003 Red Sox gave new hope to their fans. While Pedro Martinez, Manny Ramirez and Nomar Garciaparra continued to star, imports like David Ortiz, Kevin Millar and batting champ Bill Mueller helped lift the Sox to the playoffs after a three-year absence. The Red Sox, who vowed to "Cowboy Up" at the big moments, took the AL wild card and came back from an 0–2 hole to beat Oakland in the division series. They fell behind the Yankees, 3–2, in a rollicking ALCS, then won Game 6 at Yankee Stadium and led Game 7, 5–2, with one out and the bases empty in the eighth inning. But with Alan Embree and Mike Timlin ready in the bullpen, manager Grady Little stuck with a tiring Pedro Martinez until the Yankees had tied the score. Tim Wakefield, who had two victories in the series, allowed a leadoff homer to Aaron Boone in the eleventh inning, clinching the pennant for New York. It was a bitter ending for Boston, but sweet revenge was just a year away.

Tim Wakefield

RED SOX SUPERLATIVES

Whittling down the greatest moments and individual performances in the storied history of the Red Sox is a nearly impossible task, but some highlights leap to mind when assessing the franchise's remarkable history.

The Greatest Moments

GAME 6 AND THE FISK HOMER, 1975

It is, to many, the greatest game ever played. The sixth game of the 1975 World Series followed three days of rain and was worth every bit of the wait. The sheer force of competition, apart from the winning and losing, made it purely exhilarating. As the Reds' Pete Rose famously said to Sox catcher Carlton Fisk in the tenth inning that night, "This is some kind of game." Fisk agreed, and that was before his game-ending homer off the left field foul pole in the bottom of the twelfth won it for the Sox, 7–6. The rainouts had allowed the Sox to start ace Luis Tiant, but the Reds scored six runs off him and held a 6–3 lead in the eighth. With two out and two on, just after a hideous swing on a weak foul ball, Bernie Carbo launched a game-tying, pinch-hit homer into the center field seats. Dwight Evans made a game-saving catch in the eleventh to rob Joe Morgan in the right field corner, and Fisk led off the twelfth with his epic blast off Pat Darcy. The NBC camera stationed in the Green Monster followed Fisk's historic trot as he frantically waved the ball fair, clapping and dancing up the first base line. The cameraman was actually under orders to follow the flight of the ball, not the reaction of the batter, but a rat in the Wall distracted him and he could not raise his camera. It made for the unforgettable image of an unforgettable game. It was all so perfect, except for one thing: for the Red Sox, it was one game too soon. They lost Game 7, 4–3.

GAME 5, 1986 ALCS

The night before, the Red Sox had blown a three-run lead in the ninth inning of Game 4, allowing the Angels to take a commanding 3–1 lead in the ALCS. In Game 5, center fielder Dave Henderson knocked Bobby Grich's sixth-inning fly ball over the fence for a tie-breaking, two-run homer. It had all the makings of another inglorious ending for the Red Sox, until a miracle ninth-inning rally that actually started with a leadoff single by Bill Buckner. Don Baylor's one-out homer pulled the Sox within a run, at 5–4, and with two outs, Gary Lucas hit Rich Gedman with a pitch. Donnie Moore replaced Lucas and came within a strike of clinching the Angels' first pennant. But Henderson, who had homered just once in 36 regular-season games for Boston, crushed a two-run home run that put the Red Sox ahead, 6–5. The Angels tied it in the bottom of the ninth, but Steve Crawford kept the game tied by working out of a bases-loaded, one-out jam. Henderson's sacrifice fly in the 11th put the Red Sox ahead for good, at 7–6, and they blitzed the Angels in two games at Fenway to capture the pennant.

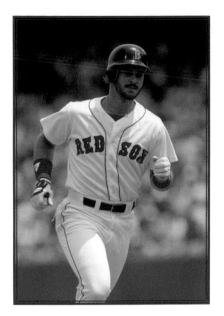

THE 1988 STRETCH DRIVE

The Red Sox had stagnated after the 1986 World Series, falling to fifth place in '87 and sleepwalking through the first half in '88. They were 43–42 at the All-Star break, nine games out of first place in the East. Then Walpole Joe Morgan took over for John McNamara, and everything changed. In Morgan's third game as manager, on July 16, the Sox overcame a 6–0 deficit to beat the Royals on a walk-off homer by Kevin Romine, who had never homered before and would hit just four more in his career. The Sox won 19 of their first 20 games under Morgan to make up the deficit and pull into a tie for first with Detroit. With Morgan playing hunches to brilliant effect, the Sox went on an 11–3 tear in mid-September to all but lock up the AL East. Roger Clemens and Bruce Hurst won 18 games each, and Mike Greenwell hit .325 with 22 homers and 119 RBIs, finishing as the runner-up in the MVP race. The Sox would be runners-up for the pennant, too—they were swept in the ALCS by the Oakland A's.

Great Individual Performances

CY YOUNG'S PERFECT GAME, 1904

Cy Young holds many records, but few as obscure as this one: most consecutive hitless innings, 24. Before his start on May 5, 1904, against the Philadelphia Athletics at Huntington Avenue Grounds, Young had thrown nine no-hit innings over two games. After his perfect game, the first in AL history, he notched six more no-hit innings. It is just another part of Young's almost inconceivable career. This game was the obvious gem of his 511 victories. In the first perfect game to be thrown by a pitcher standing 60 feet, 6 inches from the plate, Young retired the opposing pitcher, Hall of Famer Rube Waddell, on a fly out to center for the final out.

ERNIE SHORE'S PERFECT GAME, 1917

This is the perfect game with an asterisk attached. On June 23, 1917, a hotheaded Red Sox lefty named Babe Ruth walked the leadoff hitter, Ray Morgan, in a game against the Washington Senators. The umpire, Brick Owens, ejected Ruth for arguing the calls and threatening him physically. Into the game came Ernie Shore, who had played with Ruth on a Baltimore farm club and been sold to Boston on the same day, in 1914. Morgan was promptly caught stealing, and Shore retired the next 26 hitters in a 4–0 Boston victory. Only Cy Young in 1904 and Addie Joss in 1908 had pitched perfect games before Shore's, and while his was not, technically, a perfect game, it was certainly the only game of its kind in baseball history.

WILLIAMS HITS .406

It was September 28, 1941, and Ted Williams was batting .400 ... just .400. His average had not slipped below that level since July 24, and the Red Sox manager, Joe Cronin, suggested Williams sit out the season-ending double-header that day in Philadelphia. His average would be frozen—technically .3996, which would be rounded up to .400—and Williams would become the first .400 hitter since Bill Terry in 1930. Williams refused Cronin's offer and smacked 6 hits in 8 at-bats that day, finishing at .406. No player has topped .400 since. Williams' feat was somewhat overshadowed that season by Joe DiMaggio's record 56-game hitting streak for the Yankees. But in 1991, the 50th anniversary of their magical shared summer, DiMaggio paid Williams the ultimate compliment: "He was the best pure hitter I ever saw," he said.

WILLIAMS' TWO TRIPLE CROWNS

Only eight players in history have led the American League in batting average, home runs and RBIs in the same season. All of these Triple Crown winners are in the Hall of Fame—but only Ted Williams did it twice. In 1942, the year after he hit .406, Williams hit .356 with 36 homers and 137 RBIs for his first Triple Crown. In 1947, he pulled it off again, at .343-32-114. Incredibly, Williams did not win the MVP award in either season. Joe Gordon won in 1942, and Joe DiMaggio won by a single point in 1947; one writer left Williams off his 10-man ballot in '47, costing Williams the award. Despite his adversarial relationship with the press, Williams did win two MVPs, in 1946 and 1949.

YAZ'S TRIPLE CROWN

In 1967, America learned how to pronounce Yastrzemski. There was no avoiding it. Carl Yastrzemski already had a batting title to his name, but he had never come close to the American League lead in homers or runs batted in. In '67, though, when the Red Sox needed him most, Yastrzemski responded with a torrid stretch run, lifting his team to the World Series and capturing the Triple Crown for himself. In the last 12 games of the season, Yastrzemski hit .523 (23-for-44) with five homers and 16 RBIs as the Red Sox held off three rivals to win their first pennant in 21 years. Yaz finished at .326, with career highs in homers (44, tied with Harmon Killebrew) and RBIs (121). No player has won the Triple Crown since.

CLEMENS' 20-STRIKEOUT GAMES

Ten years apart—on his way to stardom and on his way out of town—Roger Clemens did something no pitcher had ever done before. He struck out 20 batters in a nine-inning game, and did so both times without a walk. The first game heralded Clemens's arrival as a superstar. It was April 29, 1986, and Clemens nearly missed the start. The Celtics were hosting a playoff game that night, and Clemens got caught in a traffic snarl on Storrow Drive. He left his car and popped the trunk, planning to switch into sneakers and jog to Fenway. A police officer approached, recognized Clemens, and cleared a path for him to the game. The Red Sox had another starter ready, but Clemens insisted on pitching and vaulted into history in a 3–1 victory over the Mariners. He tied his own record on Sept. 18, 1996, in Detroit, in his final victory for the Red Sox. Clemens was concentrating on getting the victory and the shutout, which would tie him with Cy Young for the club record in both categories. When he whiffed Travis Fryman on a splitter to win, 4–0, catcher Bill Haselman bounced to the mound to congratulate him. "We tied the big man," Clemens told his catcher, referring to Cy Young. Haselman told Clemens he had also tied the record of another big man—himself.

PEDRO MARTINEZ'S 1999 PLAYOFF GAME AT CLEVELAND

Starting with the infamous Bill Buckner gaffe in the 1986 World Series, the Red Sox had lost 16 of 17 postseason games before their 1999 division series with the Cleveland Indians. So what happened in Game 1? Pedro Martinez, who had gone 23–4 to win the first of two Cy Young awards with the Sox, went down with a back injury after four innings. The Sox lost the first two games but rallied to win the next two at Fenway, setting up a high-flying finale at Jacobs Field. Martinez could not start it, but with the score tied at 8–8 in the fourth inning, someone had to restore order. In came Martinez to stifle the best offense in baseball, despite the sore back. He worked six no-hit innings as the Red Sox won the game and the series. Troy O'Leary smoked two homers, including a grand slam, to lead the offense, but this was Martinez's masterpiece.

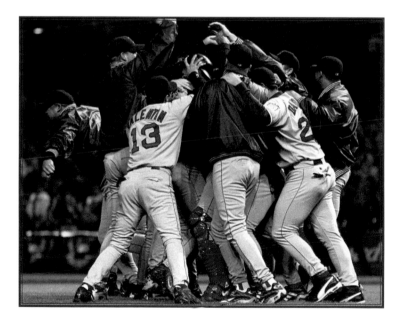

TALKIN' RED SOX BASEBALL

"A man has to have goals—for a day, for a lifetime—and that was mine: to have people say, 'There goes Ted Williams, the greatest hitter who ever lived.'" TED WILLIAMS

"Baseball isn't a life-and-death matter, but the Red Sox are." MIKE BARNICLE, THE *BOSTON GLOBE*, 1977

"Fenway Park, in Boston, is a lyric little bandbox of a ballpark. *Everything is painted green and seems in curiously sharp focus, like the inside of an old-fashioned peeping-type Easter egg."* JOHN UPDIKE, "HUB FANS BID KID ADIEU," THE NEW YORKER, 1960

"There's nothing in the world like the fatalism of Red Sox fans, *which has been bred into them for generations by that little green ballpark, and by the Wall, and by a team that keeps trying to win by hitting everything out of sight and just out-bombing everyone else in the league."* BILL LEE, TO ROGER ANGELL IN LATE INNINGS

"If I have my choice between a pennant and a Triple Crown, I'll take the pennant every time." CARL YASTRZEMSKI

"My clearest memory comes from my youngest son, Owen. *In '86 he was nine, and he came down for the third game of the World Series. Oil Can Boyd pitched the game and we lost ... As we left the ballpark, he started to cry. I said, 'Now you're a Red Sox fan.'"* NOVELIST STEPHEN KING

"I like Boston and the Boston fans. They have treated me splendidly, and if not for Frazee, I would be content to play with the Red Sox to the end of my baseball days. Boston seems more or less like my hometown, and with a regular man at the head of the club, I would prefer to remain there. Frazee sold me because he was unwilling to meet my demands and to alibi himself with the fans, he is trying to throw the blame on me." BABE RUTH, AFTER OWNER HARRY FRAZEE SOLD HIM TO THE YANKEES IN 1920

"Roger has a terrific level of concentration, focus, and exceptional work habits, which has led to excellence over a long period of time."
HALL OF FAMER TOM SEAVER

"They say John held the ball. He didn't. He was blind to what was happening, deaf to his teammates, and he made a normal play. Slaughter made a great play. If Dominic is out there in center, Slaughter stays on third base. Period."
BOBBY DOERR, AS QUOTED BY DAVID HALBERSTAM IN *THE TEAMMATES*, ON THE DECISIVE PLAY IN GAME 7 OF THE 1946 WORLD SERIES

"I tell you, one day I was driving from my house to the stadium on a workout day, and I saw a big sign on the street that said, 'Keep the Faith.' And I saw it was a photo of Manny, it had the big smile. I just parked in front of the photo and I just sat down for a minute and just thought about it—you know, we've been through the whole year. Then I went to the field and I just expressed myself to my teammates about what the Boston nation has been waiting for us and what they expect from us. So it doesn't matter if we are down 3-0. We just have got to keep the faith." DAVID ORTIZ, AFTER THE RED SOX COMPLETED THEIR HISTORIC COMEBACK OVER THE YANKEES IN THE 2004 ALCS*

"We can't reverse what was a long time ago. I'm sure there are a lot of people in New England that are dancing in the streets right now. For that, I'm thrilled. I can't wait to go back and join them." MANAGER TERRY FRANCONA, AFTER THE RED SOX WON THE 2004 WORLD SERIES IN ST. LOUIS

"And all of a sudden the ball was there, like the Mystic River Bridge, suspended out in the black of the morning." PETER GAMMONS, DESCRIBING CARLTON FISK'S FAMOUS HOMER IN THE LEAD OF HIS GAME STORY IN THE *BOSTON GLOBE,* OCT. 22, 1975

"I don't care about damn curses. Wake up the damn Bambino
and have me face him. Maybe I'll drill him in the ass, pardon me the word." PEDRO
MARTINEZ, 2001

"Lonborg and Champagne." MANAGER DICK WILLIAMS, WHEN ASKED FOR HIS PLANS FOR GAME 7 OF THE 1967 WORLD SERIES. HE DID START JIM LONBORG, BUT THE CARDINALS DRANK THE CHAMPAGNE

"He believed in me—a little, scrawny, skinny kid from Tampa, Florida. He saw something that a lot of other people passed up on." WADE BOGGS REFERRING TO GEORGE DIGBY, THE RED SOX SCOUT WHO SIGNED HIM, AT HIS HALL OF FAME SPEECH IN 2005

"The 1-0 pitch, here it is. Swing and a ground ball—stabbed by Foulke! He has it! He underhands to first and the Boston Red Sox are the world champions! For the first time in 86 years, the Red Sox have won baseball's world championship. Can you believe it?" JOE CASTIGLIONE'S CALL OF THE LAST OUT OF THE 2004 WORLD SERIES

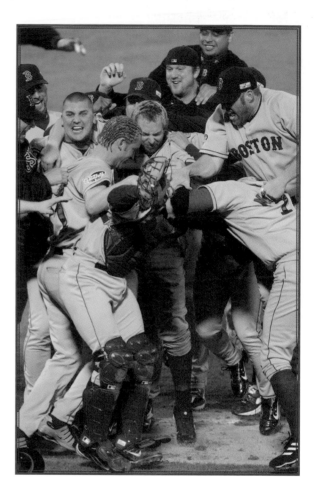

"I know I'm going to live long enough when we're gonna be world champions." RED SOX LEGEND JOHNNY PESKY— CONGRATULATIONS, JOHNNY, YOU MADE IT

THE RIVALRY

Boston vs. New York

In the euphoria of the post-game celebration after the Red Sox won the 2004 World Series in St. Louis, someone called out to team president Larry Lucchino that the Red Sox had won as many championships as the Yankees in the 21st century. Lucchino objected.

"They won in the last century, though," said Lucchino, who was somehow still dry in the wild visitors' locker room after Game 4.

"2000 was part of the last century." Then a well-wisher ambushed Lucchino from behind, dumping champagne on his head.

Not only did the Red Sox win a World Series before the Yankees this century, but they also left their rivals in their wake while doing it. The Red Sox, who could always be counted on to raise and dash their fans' hopes, pulled off the greatest comeback in postseason

There was no love lost between Yankee captain Thurman Munson and Red Sox icon Carlton Fisk.

history at the expense of the Yankees, recovering from a three-games-to-none deficit to win the ALCS at Yankee Stadium. Then they swept the Cardinals in the World Series.

Even so, it is highly unlikely any team could ever catch the Yankees for most championships. New York has won 26, all since buying Babe Ruth from the Red Sox in 1920. While the Yankees were winning those titles, the Red Sox did not win any. In that sense, it was as much of a rivalry as windshield versus bug.

But that dynamic—bullies versus bridesmaids—has made the Red Sox-Yankees rivalry so special. And it stems from the fact that the Red Sox virtually gave away their championship karma to the Yankees.

The Red Sox won five of the first 15 World Series through 1918. The Yankees, in those same years, had just five winning seasons. But the price of success caught up with the Red Sox. When Tris Speaker wanted a raise in 1916, he was sold to Cleveland. Harry Frazee, a New Yorker who financed Broadway shows, bought the team late that year and continued the trend.

In July 1919, Carl Mays, an ace pitcher on the 1918 champs, was off to a 5–11 start. Frazee shipped him to the Yankees for $40,000 and two players. The Red Sox finished in sixth place despite a record-breaking 29 homers from Ruth, who ditched the team on the last weekend of the season to make money playing in an exhibition game.

Still, Ruth was the greatest star in baseball, and he felt underpaid after signing a three-year, $30,000 contract before the 1919 season. He wanted $20,000 for 1920, and Frazee balked. On Jan. 3, 1920, he sold Ruth to the Yankees for $125,000 and a $350,000 loan against the mortgage on Fenway Park.

"With this money, the Boston club can now go into the market and buy other players and have a stronger and better team," Frazee decreed after the deal. He added that he and the Boston fans wanted a winning team, "rather than a one-man team which finishes in sixth place."

What the Red Sox got, instead, was a streak of 15 seasons without a winning record, and, of course, 86 seasons without a championship. Frazee's attention shifted more and more to Broadway, and he opened "No, No, Nanette"— the play often cited as the reason he needed cash—in 1923.

Ruth was not the only gift the Red Sox bestowed on Yankees owner Jacob Ruppert.

Frazee and Ruppert had a common bond in their opposition to AL president Ban Johnson, and continued making deals with each other. Other disastrous sales would follow: Waite Hoyt in Dec. 1920, Herb Pennock in Jan. 1923 and, after Frazee had sold the team, Red Ruffing in 1930. All three pitchers were mediocre, at best, with the Red Sox and turned into Hall of Famers in pinstripes.

By the 2000s, the teams had virtually stopped trading with each other, though there was one memorable deal between the early years and the modern era. In 1972, the Red Sox sent left-handed reliever Sparky Lyle to the Yankees for infielders Danny Cater and Mario Guerrero. Lyle saved 35 games for the Yankees that season and won the Cy Young Award in 1977, helping the Yankees to a World Series title.

By then the Yankees were playing in a remodeled version of Yankee Stadium. The original had opened on April 18, 1923, with the Yankees downing the Red Sox, 4–1, as Ruth hit the first home run. Frazee sat with Ruppert at the game.

The Red Sox were a laughingstock at the time, and would not recover until the late 1930s. Even then, the Yankees never let them get too close to the pennant. Boston finished second to the Yankees in 1938, 1939, 1941 and 1942, but the Yankees won the pennant by at least nine games each time.

The personal rivalry between Ted Williams of the Red Sox and Joe DiMaggio of the Yankees spiced the teams' rivalry in those seasons.

Both accomplished their most memorable feats in the same season, 1941, with DiMaggio's 56-game hitting streak coinciding with Williams' .406 average. The stately DiMaggio, who discouraged comparisons to the temperamental Williams, won the MVP.

In '49, the Yankees beat the Red Sox on the last two days of the regular season to capture the AL pennant by a game over Boston. Thus began a string of 17 seasons in which the Yankees finished ahead of the Red Sox in the standings.

By the mid-1970s, finally, both teams were competitive at the same time again. Fans debated which catcher was better—Boston's Carlton Fisk or New York's Thurman Munson—and players sensed a bitterness to the rivalry. There were brawls: one sparked by Fisk and Munson in '73, another in '76 in which Bill Lee separated his shoulder in a scrum with Graig Nettles. And, of course, there was 1978, which amounted to a season-long brawl.

That was the season the Yankees stormed from 14 games back in July to steal the AL East flag in a one-game playoff at Fenway Park. Maybe it was bad karma: the Red Sox

pitcher who gave up Bucky Dent's back-breaking three-run homer, Mike Torrez, had thrown the final pitch of the World Series for the Yankees the year before.

The rivalry reached another peak again in the late 1990s. In '98, the teams began an unprecedented streak in baseball history of one team finishing second to another. Through 2005, the Yankees and Sox had finished 1-2 in the AL East for eight consecutive seasons.

Of course, the introduction of the wild card made it possible to finish second and get another shot at the division winner in October. The Red Sox took advantage in 1999, 2003 and 2004, meeting the Yankees in the ALCS in each of those seasons.

In '99, the Sox made it despite losing Mo Vaughn as a free agent the year before. They got a season for the ages from Pedro Martinez, whose wizardry included a one-hitter with 17 strikeouts and no walks at Yankee Stadium on Sept. 10.

But Martinez could not pitch until the third game of the ALCS, having tossed six no-hit innings of relief to close out the Indians in Game 5 of the division series. By the time Martinez took the mound, the Sox had lost the first two games at Yankee Stadium. He would win Game 3, but the Yankees won the next two handily on their way to their 25th championship.

By 2003, the Sox had retooled under new owners John Henry, Tom Werner and Larry Lucchino. The group brought a plucky, fighting spirit to the rivalry, and when the Yankees outbid the Red Sox for pitcher Jose Contreras in 2002, Lucchino was not afraid to dub the Yankees "the evil empire" in an interview with the *New York Times*' Murray Chass.

The nickname enraged Yankees owner George Steinbrenner, but he would have the last laugh the next October. Down to their final five outs and trailing by three runs in Game 7 of the ALCS, the Yankees rallied to tie it off Martinez, and won the pennant on Aaron Boone's home run in the 11th inning.

The teams had played 26 games overall in 2003—including 19 in the regular season—and would meet the same number of times in 2004. There was so much hype for the rivalry that spring-training games became a happening, with commemorative pins selling for $6 at City of Palms Park in Fort Myers.

The season did not disappoint. Newcomers Alex Rodriguez of the Yankees and Curt

Schilling of the Red Sox added spark with their play and their personality, which grated on the other team. There was a brawl in July and another inevitable October confrontation.

The story of that skirmish will be passed down for generations in Boston: Down 3–0 in the American League Championship Series, three outs from a sweep ... Dave Roberts' dash around the bases in Game 4... David Ortiz' walk-off heroics in Games 4 and 5 ... Schilling's bloody sock in Game 6... the blowout in Game 7.

"Nothing happens easily for the Red Sox," Johnny Damon said after winning the pennant, and he was right, of course. Babe Ruth's curse had been extraordinary, and it took an extraordinary effort to reverse it.

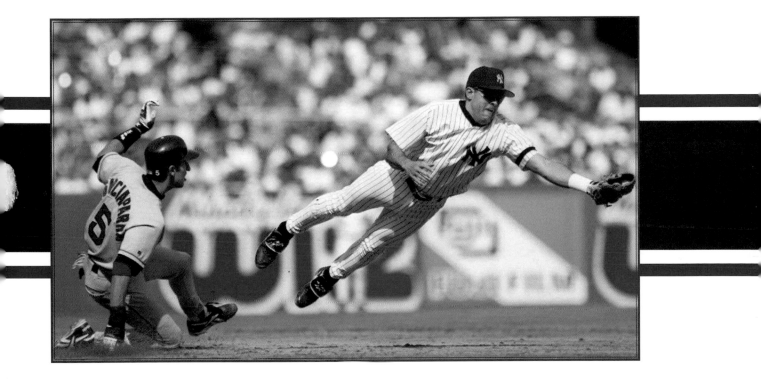

Carl Yastrzemski

FACTS AND FIGURES

Red Sox Statistical Leaders
CAREER

BATTING AVERAGE

RANK	PLAYER	AVG
1.	Ted Williams	.344
2.	Wade Boggs	.338
3.	Tris Speaker	.337
4.	Nomar Garciaparra	.323
5.	Jimmie Foxx	.320

HOME RUNS

RANK	PLAYER	HRs
1.	Ted Williams	521
2.	Carl Yastrzemski	452
3.	Jim Rice	382
4.	Dwight Evans	379
5.	Mo Vaughn	230

RBIs

RANK	PLAYER	RBIs
1.	Carl Yastrzemski	1,844
2.	Ted Williams	1,839
3.	Jim Rice	1,451
4.	Dwight Evans	1,346
5.	Bobby Doerr	1,247

RUNS

RANK	PLAYER	RUNS
1.	Carl Yastrzemski	1,816
2.	Ted Williams	1,798
3.	Dwight Evans	1,435
4.	Jim Rice	1,249
5.	Bobby Doerr	1,094

STOLEN BASES

RANK	PLAYER	SBs
1.	Harry Hooper	300
2.	Tris Speaker	267
3.	Carl Yastrzemski	168
4.	Heinie Wagner	141
5.	Larry Gardner	134

SLUGGING

RANK	PLAYER	PCT.
1.	Ted Williams	.634
2.	Manny Ramirez	.608
3.	Jimmie Foxx	.605
4.	David Ortiz	.600
5.	Nomar Garciaparra	.553

OPS

RANK	PLAYER	PCT.
1.	Ted Williams	1.115
2.	Jimmie Foxx	1.034
3.	Manny Ramirez	1.020
4.	Mo Vaughn	.936
5.	Nomar Garciaparra	.923

GAMES

RANK	PLAYER	GAMES
1.	Carl Yastrzemski	3,308
2.	Dwight Evans	2,505
3.	Ted Williams	2,292
4.	Jim Rice	2,089
5.	Bobby Doerr	1,865

Manny Ramirez

WINS

RANK	PLAYER	WINs
1.	Roger Clemens	192
	Cy Young	192
3.	Tim Wakefield	130
4.	Mel Parnell	123
5.	Luis Tiant	122

ERA

RANK	PLAYER	ERA
1.	Joe Wood	1.99
2.	Cy Young	2.00
3.	Dutch Leonard	2.13
4.	Babe Ruth	2.19
5.	Carl Mays	2.21

STRIKEOUTS

RANK	PLAYER	Ks
1.	Roger Clemens	2,590
2.	Pedro Martinez	1,683
3.	Tim Wakefield	1,480
4.	Cy Young	1,341
5.	Luis Tiant	1,075

SAVES

RANK	PLAYER	SAVES
1.	Bob Stanley	132
2.	Dick Radatz	104
3.	Ellis Kinder	91
4.	Jeff Reardon	88
5.	Derek Lowe	85

Cy Young

Red Sox Statistical Leaders
SINGLE SEASON

BATTING AVG

RANK	PLAYER	AVG	YEAR
1.	Ted Williams	.406	1941
2.	Ted Williams	.388	1957
3.	Tris Speaker	.383	1912
4.	Nomar Garciaparra	.372	2000
5.	Dale Alexander	.372	1932

HOME RUNS

RANK	PLAYER	HR	YEAR
1.	Jimmie Foxx	50	1938
2.	David Ortiz	47	2005
3.	Jim Rice	46	1978
4.	Manny Ramirez	45	2005
5.	Mo Vaughn	44	1996
	Carl Yastrzemski	44	1967

RBIs

RANK	PLAYER	RBIs	YEAR
1.	Jimmie Foxx	175	1938
2.	Vern Stephens	159	1949
	Ted Williams	159	1949
4.	David Ortiz	148	2005
5.	Ted Williams	145	1939

RUNS

RANK	PLAYER	RUNS	YEAR
1.	Ted Williams	150	1949
2.	Ted Williams	142	1946
3.	Ted Williams	141	1942
4.	Jimmie Foxx	139	1938
5.	Tris Speaker	136	1912

Jimmie Foxx

STOLEN BASES

RANK	PLAYER	SBs	YEAR
1.	Tommy Harper	54	1973
2.	Tris Speaker	52	1912
3.	Tris Speaker	46	1913
4.	Otis Nixon	42	1994
	Tris Speaker	42	1914

SLUGGING

RANK	PLAYER	PCT	YEAR
1.	Ted Williams	.735	1941
2.	Ted Williams	.731	1957
3.	Jimmie Foxx	.704	1938
4.	Jimmie Foxx	.694	1939
5.	Ted Williams	.667	1946

OPS

RANK	PLAYER	PCT	YEAR
1.	Ted Williams	1.287	1941
2.	Ted Williams	1.257	1957
3.	Jimmie Foxx	1.166	1938
4.	Ted Williams	1.164	1946
5.	Jimmie Foxx	1.158	1939

WINS

RANK	PLAYER	WINS	YEAR
1.	Joe Wood	34	1912
2.	Cy Young	33	1901
3.	Cy Young	32	1902
4.	Cy Young	28	1903
5.	Cy Young	26	1904

ERA

RANK	PLAYER	PCT	YEAR
1.	Dutch Leonard	0.96	1914
2.	Cy Young	1.26	1908
3.	Ray Collins	1.62	1910
4.	Cy Young	1.62	1901
5.	Ernie Shore	1.64	1915

STRIKEOUTS

RANK	PLAYER	Ks	YEAR
1.	Pedro Martinez	313	1999
2.	Roger Clemens	291	1988
3.	Pedro Martinez	284	2000
4.	Joe Wood	258	1912
5.	Roger Clemens	257	1996

SAVES

RANK	PLAYER	SAVES	YEAR
1.	Tom Gordon	46	1998
2.	Derek Lowe	42	2000
3.	Jeff Reardon	40	1991
	Ugueth Urbina	40	2002
5.	Jeff Russell	33	1993
	Bob Stanley	33	1983

Retired Numbers

No.	PLAYER
1	Bobby Doerr
4	Joe Cronin
8	Carl Yastrzemski
9	Ted Williams
27	Carlton Fisk
42	Jackie Robinson*

*Retired by all major league clubs

MVPs

PLAYER	YEAR
Mo Vaughn	1995
Roger Clemens	1986
Jim Rice	1978
Fred Lynn	1975
Carl Yastrzemski	1967
Jackie Jensen	1958
Ted Williams	1949
Ted Williams	1946
Jimmie Foxx	1938

Mo Vaughn

Pedro Martinez

Cy Young Award Winners

PLAYER	YEAR
Pedro Martinez	2000
Pedro Martinez	1999
Roger Clemens	1991
Roger Clemens	1987
Roger Clemens	1986
Jim Lonborg	1967

Rookies of the Year

PLAYER	YEAR
Nomar Garciaparra	1997
Fred Lynn	1975
Carlton Fisk	1972
Don Schwall	1961
Walt Dropo	1950

Triple Crown

PLAYER	YEAR
Carl Yastrzemski	1967
Ted Williams	1947
Ted Williams	1942

Year-by-Year Results

YEAR	W	L	PCT	GB	MANAGER
2005	95	67	.586	-	Terry Francona
2004	98	64	.605	3.0	Terry Francona
2003	95	67	.586	6.0	Grady Little
2002	93	69	.574	10.5	Grady Little
2001	82	79	.509	13.5	Jimy Williams/Joe Kerrigan
2000	85	77	.525	2.5	Jimy Williams
1999	94	68	.580	4.0	Jimy Williams
1998	92	70	.568	22.0	Jimy Williams
1997	78	84	.481	20.0	Jimy Williams
1996	85	77	.525	7.0	Kevin Kennedy
1995	86	58	.597	-	Kevin Kennedy
1994	54	61	.470	17.0	Butch Hobson
1993	80	82	.494	15.0	Butch Hobson
1992	73	89	.451	23.0	Butch Hobson
1991	84	78	.519	7.0	Joe Morgan
1990	88	74	.543	-	Joe Morgan
1989	83	79	.512	6.0	Joe Morgan
1988	89	73	.549	-	John McNamara/Joe Morgan
1987	78	84	.481	20.0	John McNamara
1986	95	66	.590	-	John McNamara
1985	81	81	.500	18.5	John McNamara
1984	86	76	.531	18.0	Ralph Houk
1983	78	84	.481	20.0	Ralph Houk

1982	89	73	.549	6.0	Ralph Houk
1981	59	49	.546	2.5	Ralph Houk
1980	83	77	.519	19.0	Don Zimmer/Johnny Pesky
1979	91	69	.569	11.5	Don Zimmer
1978	99	64	.607	1.0	Don Zimmer
1977	97	64	.602	2.5	Don Zimmer
1976	83	79	.512	15.5	Darrell Johnson/Don Zimmer
1975	95	65	.594	-	Darrell Johnson
1974	84	78	.519	7.0	Darrell Johnson
1973	89	73	.549	8.0	Eddie Kasko/Eddie Popowski
1972	85	70	.548	0.5	Eddie Kasko
1971	85	77	.525	18.0	Eddie Kasko
1970	87	75	.537	21.0	Eddie Kasko
1969	87	75	.537	22.0	Dick Williams/Eddie Popowski
1968	86	76	.531	17.0	Dick Williams
1967	92	70	.568	-	Dick Williams
1966	72	90	.444	26.0	Billy Herman/Pete Runnels
1965	62	100	.383	40.0	Billy Herman
1964	72	90	.444	27.0	Johnny Pesky/Billy Herman
1963	76	85	.472	28.0	Johnny Pesky
1962	76	84	.475	19.0	Pinky Higgins
1961	76	86	.469	33.0	Pinky Higgins
1960	65	89	.422	32.0	Billy Jurges/Del Baker/Pinky Higgins
1959	75	79	.487	19.0	Pinky Higgins/Rudy York/Billy Jurges
1958	79	75	.513	13.0	Pinky Higgins

1957	82	72	.532	16.0	Pinky Higgins
1956	84	70	.545	13.0	Pinky Higgins
1955	84	70	.545	12.0	Pinky Higgins
1954	69	85	.448	42.0	Lou Boudreau
1953	84	69	.549	16.0	Lou Boudreau
1952	76	78	.494	19.0	Lou Boudreau
1951	87	67	.565	11.0	Steve O'Neill
1950	94	60	.610	4.0	Joe McCarthy/Steve O'Neill
1949	96	58	.623	1.0	Joe McCarthy
1948	96	59	.619	1.0	Joe McCarthy
1947	83	71	.539	14.0	Joe Cronin
1946	104	50	.675	-	Joe Cronin
1945	71	83	.461	17.5	Joe Cronin
1944	77	77	.500	12.0	Joe Cronin
1943	68	84	.447	29.0	Joe Cronin
1942	93	59	.612	9.0	Joe Cronin
1941	84	70	.545	17.0	Joe Cronin
1940	82	72	.532	8.0	Joe Cronin
1939	89	62	.589	17.0	Joe Cronin
1938	88	61	.591	9.5	Joe Cronin
1937	80	72	.526	21.0	Joe Cronin
1936	74	80	.481	28.5	Joe Cronin
1935	78	75	.510	16.0	Joe Cronin
1934	76	76	.500	24.0	Bucky Harris
1933	63	86	.423	34.5	Marty McManus
1932	43	111	.279	64.0	Shano Collins/Marty McManus
1931	62	90	.408	45.0	Shano Collins
1930	52	102	.338	50.0	Heinie Wagner
1929	58	96	.377	48.0	Bill Carrigan

1928	57	96	.373	43.5	Bill Carrigan
1927	51	103	.331	59.0	Bill Carrigan
1926	46	107	.301	44.5	Lee Fohl
1925	47	105	.309	49.5	Lee Fohl
1924	67	87	.435	25.0	Lee Fohl
1923	61	91	.401	37.0	Frank Chance
1922	61	93	.396	33.0	Hugh Duffy
1921	75	79	.487	23.5	Hugh Duffy
1920	72	81	.471	25.5	Ed Barrow
1919	66	71	.482	20.5	Ed Barrow
1918	75	51	.595	-	Ed Barrow
1917	90	62	.592	9.0	Jack Barry
1916	91	63	.591	-	Bill Carrigan
1915	101	50	.669	-	Bill Carrigan
1914	91	62	.595	8.5	Bill Carrigan
1913	79	71	.527	15.5	Jake Stahl/Bill Carrigan
1912	105	47	.691	-	Jake Stahl
1911	78	75	.510	24.0	Patsy Donovan
1910	81	72	.529	22.5	Patsy Donovan
1909	88	63	.583	9.5	Fred Lake
1908	75	79	.487	15.5	Deacon McGuire/Fred Lake
1907	59	90	.396	32.5	Cy Young/George Huff/Bob Unglaub/ Deacon McGuire
1906	49	105	.318	45.5	Jimmy Collins/Chuck Stahl
1905	78	74	.513	16.0	Jimmy Collins
1904	95	59	.617	-	Jimmy Collins
1903	91	47	.659	-	Jimmy Collins
1902	77	60	.562	6.5	Jimmy Collins
1901	79	57	.581	4.0	Jimmy Collins